D.J. CLARK

GOD GIVES YOU THE DOG YOU NEED

*Life Lessons My Dogs
(and a Few Others) Taught Me*

TRILOGY

PROFESSIONAL PUBLISHING MEETS POWERFUL PROMOTION

A wholly owned subsidiary of TBN

DEDICATION

This book is dedicated to God first. God has watched over my life, protecting me in more ways than I will ever know. I also dedicate this book to Dolores, who showed me how people can persevere and be resilient in this world. To Jack, who modeled how to care for God's creatures when he caught bees that were found inside the house and set them free outside. To Lynette, who showed me that people can have fun and still be strong and caring. And to Bob, the only person I know who did not hesitate to put an injured screech owl into the passenger seat of his car so he could take it to a veterinarian. To all my friends who give me encouragement just when I need it: You are the best! And to all the people who help animals every day, including those who work in animal hospitals and veterinary clinics; who volunteer in animal rescue groups and shelters (caring for both domesticated and wildlife animals); animal welfare officers and police officers (like those who rescued Champ); as well as the investigators, prosecutors, and all support staff who fight for justice for animals. When we are striving for justice, it can feel like it is "just us," but we can do this together.

CONTENTS

Bob and Stella

INTRODUCTION

I believe God communicates with us in many ways and that animals are valuable partners in our lives that God sends to help us. These "messengers" have a way of sharing that can seem like a miracle. These are a few of the stories I have been blessed to receive. I hope that one day all God's creatures are loved, cared for, and valued as the wonderful gifts that they are.

> *But ask the animals, and they will teach you,*
> *or the birds in the sky, and they will tell you.*
> **—Job 12:7**

Dear God, thank You for sending these wonderful dogs, cats, and people into my life to teach me what You want me to learn. I pray that You continue to send them to me throughout my entire life, to help me navigate what can be a complicated place. Amen

.

DOGS

SOLO

And we know that in all things God works for the good of those who love him, who have been called according to his purpose.

—Romans 8:28

I still remember watching our new black-and-white puppy playing after we chose him from the giant group of siblings in his litter. My dad came up with the name "Solo" because our puppy was a basset mix and because his stomach was "so low" to the ground.

Solo was a beloved member of our family and always kept us entertained with his antics. He always protected us, but I noticed that as he got older, he spent more of his time in his new favorite activity: napping on the couch. If any attempt was made to interrupt his nap, Solo would open one eye, glare at the one who dared to waken him, and growl to clearly let them know he was not going to be moved—and he was serious.

One morning when I was seventeen, I was asleep in my bedroom when I was startled by a loud noise next to my room. Because my bedroom door was shut, I was not sure what had happened. I looked at the clock and realized that my parents were at work and I was alone in the house. We had never had any problems before, so I felt safe, and I started to go back to sleep.

A few moments later, I heard Solo growling outside my closed bedroom door. I brushed it off again, thinking something must have fallen and startled him, too. But then I heard a noise that changed everything. I heard the footsteps of someone running—and Solo chasing after them!

I don't think I have ever been more afraid. I grabbed my phone and called 911. When the police arrived, they looked through the house, but the intruder was long gone. He had obviously escaped through a window that he'd left open.

After that day, I noticed a difference in Solo. He followed me around the house as if he were my personal bodyguard, and he really enjoyed his new assignment. Solo had a new youthful energy—it seemed like years had been shaved off his age. I was amazed to see the change in Solo. He now had a new purpose, and this new attitude stayed with him for the rest of his days.

This transformation in Solo showed me the importance of having a purpose in life. Everyone needs to have a purpose: a job to do or some way to make a contribution to the world. I believe Solo likely saved my life that summer day, and I think he knew it, too.

Thank You, God, for placing this hero in my life at a time when I needed him the most and for teaching me about the importance of purpose.

POKEY

Above all else, guard your heart, for everything you do flows from it.

—Proverbs 4:23

Pokey was a fluffy black-and-white poodle mix. I spotted him in a tiny cage at a local pet store and knew immediately I had to rescue him. I begged my parents until they gave in and let me run to the store and pay the ten-dollar "bail money" to gain his freedom. Pokey was sweet-natured and happily went with me everywhere I went.

I usually had a pretty good idea of where the dogs were, but one day I noticed that Pokey and Solo didn't seem to be around. I began looking for them and was surprised when I could not find them. I searched the entire house and even the backyard, and then I went outside and began searching the neighborhood block by block.

I was about three blocks into my search when I spotted both dogs. Solo looked like he was having a grand old time, and Pokey looked nervous and unsure of himself. I called out to them, hoping to bring them back home. But Solo was not about to have his adventure cut short, and in his usual independent spirit, he took off running the opposite direction. Pokey, on the other hand, ran straight over to me and right into my arms.

Thankfully, we eventually got Solo back home. I always had the feeling that Solo had been the instigator, the kingpin of this escape plan, and my sweet Pokey had been dragged along against his will.

Pokey was sweet and happy, and he had a heart of gold. He was always by my side through good times and sad times, too. I learned more than one lesson from Pokey, but he especially taught me that attitude is everything and that dogs are great partners to help navigate this life.

Thank You, God, for sending this sweet soul, Pokey, into my life to be my partner for a time and to show me that having a good attitude and guarding my heart can make a difference in this world.

ALLY

Enthusiasm without knowledge is no good; haste makes mistakes.

—Proverbs 19:2 NLT

I learned about Ally from an ad in a local paper advertising puppies for sale. She was a purebred black-and-tan German shepherd who carried herself with the composure of a princess. I think she knew that she was gorgeous. Ally was also smart—almost too smart. When Ally set her mind on something, she made a plan that guaranteed the success of her mission, which seems to be a common trait of her breed. Ally could have been a secret agent with her ability to remain patient until the "opportunity to strike" was just right.

One of the things on Ally's list of targets was butter. She would eat the entire tub of butter if she could get to it. If there was butter anywhere on the counter and she had the opportunity to snatch it, you could be sure that within seconds, that butter would be hers.

Butter was her favorite interest, but certainly not her only one. Another time her "target" was a burrito I was hoping to have for my dinner. After getting home from a long day, I set my burrito on the counter and then realized I had to go out of the house for a brief time. I was only gone a few minutes when I suddenly recognized my mistake: I had left my burrito and my "counter thief" alone together. Sure enough, I came back home to find an empty burrito wrapper and an incredibly happy German shepherd.

I learned from Ally that the success of a mission is all in the planning and that secret agents come in all sizes.

God, thank You for sending this beautiful dog into my life. Watching her navigate through her life was a true lesson in learning to prepare.

JUNIOR

Do not be conformed to this world, but be transformed by the renewal of your mind, that by testing you may discern what is the will of God, what is good and acceptable and perfect.

—Romans 12:2 ESV

Junior was a German shepherd mix who always seemed different from other dogs. He was even different from the siblings in his own litter, both in his appearance and in what he liked. All the puppies in his litter were the same black-and-tan color—including Junior—but he was the only one with long, flowing fur.

Junior had the ability to make a sound that I have never heard from another dog. It was a cooing sound, similar to what a dove or pigeon would make, not a sound you would expect to hear from a dog. He usually made this cooing sound when he was happy or sometimes when he was feeling impatient because he was not getting something that he wanted fast enough.

Junior also had a different idea about how to spend his time that began when he was a puppy. Every morning the woman who owned Junior's mom let the litter of puppies out into a large yard to run and play, but Junior always chose to stay behind, preferring to have the food bowl all to himself. Food, treats, and staying at home were Junior's favorite things, and that did not change as he got older.

Whenever we took Junior somewhere, he would seem to be interested in going at first, but it wasn't long before he would change his mind and let you know he wanted to go back home. He always seemed to be the happiest at home with his food bowl.

The lesson I learned from Junior is that everyone does not have to like the same things. It is okay to be different from the pack!

Thank You, Lord, for sharing Junior with me. It was so wonderful to see this guy make his way through life on his own terms.

CHAMP

And now these three remain: faith, hope and love. But the greatest of these is love.

—1 Corinthians 13:13 NIV

Champ joined our family in an unusual way after I heard about him recovering at a veterinary hospital. He had been rescued by some kind police officers from a heartbreaking experience of abuse. The first time I saw Champ, he was extremely underweight, and he had bandages on all his legs. He was going to be transferred to a local animal shelter, so this is when he became a member of our family. The vet guessed that Champ was a border collie–golden retriever mix and was about the same age as Junior, nine months old. We chose the name "Champ" for him because of his strength to survive what he had just been through.

During the first few months in our home, Champ did not respond to anything. He did not wag his tail, he didn't react to Junior, and he showed no interest in playing. Even after he had healed enough to have his bandages removed, it was as if Champ was frozen inside, unable to do anything, even with his puppy brother.

Champ had been in our family for about six months when I saw him make his first timid attempt to play with Junior. It was clumsy and it was awkward, but at the same time, it was so beautiful. It brought tears to my eyes to watch such a living and powerful lesson in the ability to recover from abuse.

Champ became one of the most kind and caring dogs I have ever known. If anyone in our house wasn't feeling well, Champ was always right by their side. I used to call him my "nurse dog" because he was so caring to everyone who needed love and attention. And I believe he would have unquestioningly laid down his life to protect us if it were ever needed.

Champ taught me one of the most incredible lessons I have ever witnessed: that love has the power to heal even those who could be seen as beyond help. I know it is possible to come back from abuse, because I saw it happen to Champ. He was a true champion. Champ was the very definition of love.

Thank You, God, for sending this courageous and caring dog into my life with a powerful lesson of love.

STELLA

For God gave us a spirit not of fear but of power and love and self-control.

—2 Timothy 1:7 ᴇꜱᴠ

There are so many words to describe Stella. She was beautiful, strong, sweet, and humorous, but most of all, Stella was fearless. She was confident in herself but not a bully. I have often wished I could be as fearless as my dog Stella.

Stella was a muscular puppy with deep golden fur. She was nine months old when I saw her at an animal rescue shelter. The workers there said she was a chow and golden retriever mix, and over the years I saw glimpses of the possibility of many different breeds in her makeup, including rottweiler, Labrador, and also pit bull. Stella had a majestic charisma and a stealthy way of being that gave her the presence of a lioness. She seemed excited for her future, and she did not even glance behind her as she left the shelter to begin the journey to her new home.

Stella and I loved to take long walks, even venturing out onto some long country roads where I always felt safe—as long as I was with my brave, confident girl. One sunny afternoon we were walking in a neighborhood when three dogs that were running loose spotted us before we saw them. They ran toward us growling like a pack of ravenous wolves. I was terrified, thinking we were about to meet our end.

Stella, on the other hand, had a quite different response. She did not seem frightened or even ready to fight;

instead she had an almost casual reaction to the other dogs, like, *Oh, is this what we are doing?*—as if it were some sort of intriguing game. She took a firm stance, then let out her own loud growl/bark with the authority that would have commanded the respect of a navy battleship commander. The three loose dogs came to a screeching halt, puzzled looks on their faces. They were likely confused when the intimidation tactics that usually worked did not affect Stella, who was not even the least bit intimidated by their approach.

Just then I heard someone calling the pack of three, and they quickly turned and ran off. As Stella and I watched them flee, I was in total disbelief about what had just happened. Stella just watched them go, then casually went on with her day.

The important lesson that I learned from Stella is, never let them see you sweat!

What a gift to live life with this fearless creature! Thank You, God, for letting me witness Stella's courage. She has been an inspiration to me in those times when I have needed courage.

JONESY AND BUBBLES

Jonesy and Bubbles had been together for years, and they were both older when they joined the family. Jonesy (a tan Chihuahua) was ten years old at the time, and Bubbles (a Chihuahua-pug mix) was eight when they came into my life.

JONESY

For everything there is a season, and a time for every matter under heaven.

—Ecclesiastes 3:1 ESV

Timid. I would definitely say Jonesy is timid. He doesn't have a mean bone in his body, and I don't think anyone could resist his sweet expression, his big, deerlike eyes, and ears that are almost too large for his head.

One of Jonesy's favorite things to do is to go for a walk. If he notices even the slightest hint that we are about to go for a walk, he starts running through the house making a range of noises. One of the things he never used to do, though, was bark. He would make other noises, like a yap or a whine, but he never barked, and I always wondered why. The veterinarian said that nothing was wrong with him physically, and he didn't know why Jonesy didn't bark.

Eventually I did some digging into Jonesy's background and learned that when he was just under a year old, he lived at a place that claimed to be an animal shelter, but it seemed more like a dungeon. The animals were all kept outside in crates. If the dogs ever barked, they were sprayed with water from a hose as punishment. I don't know how long Jonesy stayed there, but I believe it was this experience that made him think it was never okay to bark.

It took about three years before I finally heard a small bark from Jonesy one day when we were getting ready to go on a walk. Jonesy looked as surprised as I was to hear a bark come from his mouth. Since then, he has learned it is okay to bark, and he really seems to be getting the hang of it. Now when he is celebrating the upcoming walk, he yaps, whines, *and* barks.

The lesson I learned from Jonesy is that everyone's journey to recovery happens at their own speed and in their own time.

God, thank You for bringing this gentle little soul into my life and allowing me to see that recovery is a personalized journey.

BUBBLES

*But the L*ORD *said to Samuel, "Do not look on his appearance or on the height of his stature, because I have rejected him. For the L*ORD *sees not as man sees: man looks on the outward appearance, but the L*ORD *looks on the heart."*

—1 Samuel 16:7 ESV

Bubbles is a Chihuahua-pug mix, and even though she is only about eight inches tall, she does not seem to notice that she is small. She will tunnel through snow that is as high as she is, and she is determined to weave her way through patches of grass that are five times her height. She is willing to challenge dogs, cats, squirrels, or people, but the truth is, she is a very friendly dog. When she barks at people, they usually think she is adorable, not ferocious, but she does not seem to know that she is not as intimidating as she thinks. The sound of her deep growl does not match her size, either. Bubbles believes she is in charge of house security, and while it is true that her range of attack may only be ankle-high, I do not think she is aware of that, either.

The lesson I have learned from Bubbles is that believing in yourself is more valuable than your size or appearance.

God, thank You for showing me that the strength that comes from knowing God is with me is more important than my size, success, or anything else. You see what is in our hearts.

CATS

MISTY

Therefore encourage one another and build each other up, just as in fact you are doing.

—1 Thessalonians 5:11

Misty was a delicate gray tabby cat who was a part of our family when we had our two dogs, Solo and Pokey. She was a very independent feline who loved to explore the neighborhood. Misty was good friends with our dogs, but she would sometimes get into a brawl with other cats as they battled for control of the neighborhood territory. One of the things I found so fascinating about Misty was a strategy she used in these battles with the other cats. Misty would climb the wooden fence around our yard, then confidently jump down into the safety of our backyard with Solo and Pokey, where no cat rival would dare to follow. How brilliant of her to use her friendship with our dogs, all the time knowing that the rival cats would never take the chance to encounter Solo and Pokey!

I learned from Misty how important it is to have friends— and that those friends can make all the difference, especially in tough times.

Thank You, God, for letting me watch this delicate creature both strategize and rely on her friends, and for teaching me the importance of relying on others to help me in this life.

PEOPLE

BANJO

For he will order his angels to protect you wherever you go.

—Psalm 91:11 NLT

There was a chill in the air that night as I drove home from work just after midnight. When my car suddenly stopped working, it slowly glided to a stop at the side of the road. It was 1983, long before cell phones were a common companion, and I was wondering what I was going to do next. I looked around and saw someone in another car who seemed to notice my situation, but the way they just slowly circled around, staying at a distance, gave me an uneasy feeling.

I decided that my best option—my only option, really— was to get out of my car and run several blocks back to my employer's building. I stepped out of my car into the chilly night air, took a deep breath and a quick look around, then started to run. No one seemed to be around as my footsteps echoed off the concrete buildings, until suddenly I noticed a man standing nearby. As I drew closer to him, he called out, "Are you okay?"

I slowed down, and somehow felt that I should take a chance on this guy, so I told him about my broken-down car and how I was trying to get back to the building where I worked. To my surprise, he told me he would walk with me the rest of the way. It is extremely important to be cautious in a situation like this, but I strongly felt as though I could trust him and I agreed to have him walk with me. As we walked through the downtown blocks, he told me his name was Banjo, probably a street name. We chatted briefly as we walked, just the kind of small talk you have when you don't really know someone. When we arrived at my building, I thanked him, and we said good-bye.

I never saw Banjo again after that night. He seemed like an angel placed there to help me. I have often thought about that night and told others about it. Some people have commented that he might have been a veteran, and I think that is possible. I give thanks to God for placing Banjo there to protect me during my late-night journey.

The lesson I learned from this experience is that you never know who might step forward to help you when you need assistance. Sometimes it might be a dog, sometimes it might be a cat—and sometimes it might be someone like Banjo.

Thank You, God, for sending this angel to protect me.

AFTERWORD

God communicates with us in many ways, and it can be interesting and fun to watch for this. When I think about these lessons and about my precious dogs, who have left pawprints on my heart that have changed me forever, I think about the term *dog handler* and find it somewhat backward. Although the world might see me as my dogs' "handler," when I look back, I can see that they were equally mine.

CPSIA information can be obtained
at www.ICGtesting.com
Printed in the USA
LVHW030444040423
743339LV00003B/614